PETER PAUPER PRESS
Fine Books and Gifts Since 1928

Our Company

the age of twenty-two, Peter Beilenson began printing books
press in the basement of his parents' home in Larchmont,
Peter—and later, his wife, Edna—sought to create fine
old at "prices even a pauper could afford."

family owned and operated, Peter Pauper Press continues to
ounders' legacy—and our customers' expectations—of beauty,
value.

Visit us at www.peterpauper.com

J O U R

In 1928, a
on a smal
New York
books that

Today, stil
honor our
quality, an

PETE
WHIT

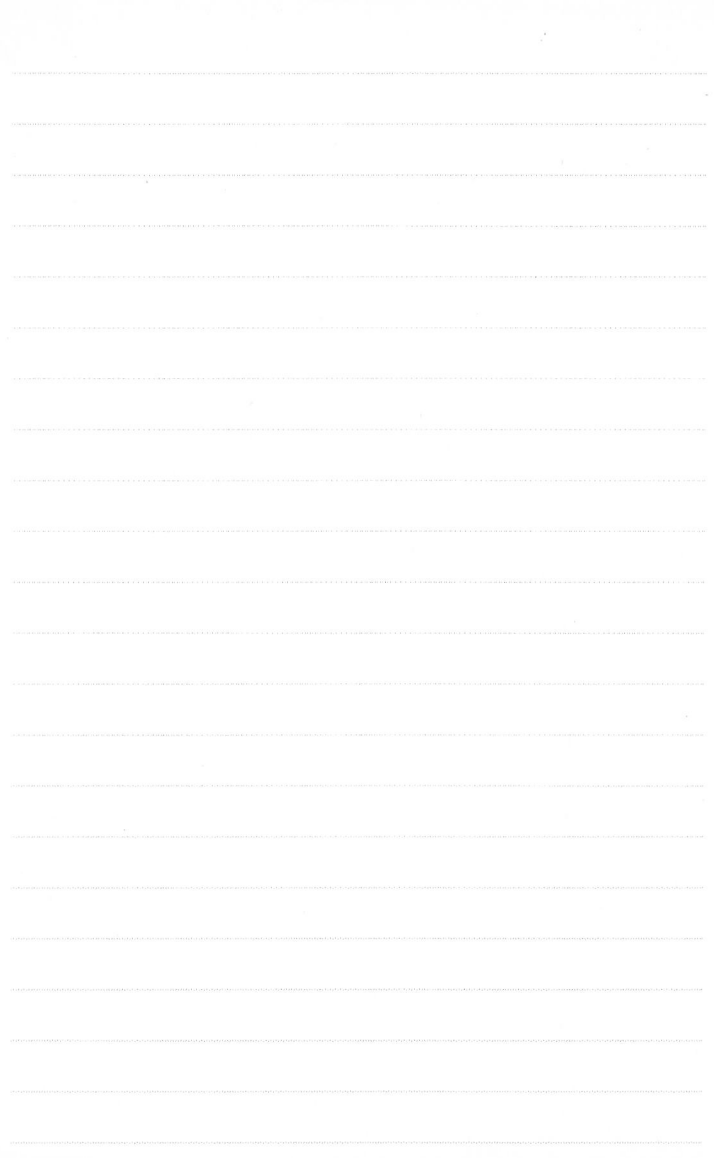